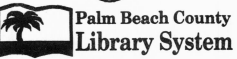

BOAS

BOAS

MARY ANN McDONALD

THE CHILD'S WORLD®, INC.

Library of Congress Cataloging-in-Publication Data
McDonald, Mary Ann
Boas / Mary Ann McDonald.
p.   cm.
Includes index.
Summary: Describes the physical characteristics, behavior, and life cycle of the boa constrictor.
ISBN 1-56766-212-9 (hard cover : library binding)
1. Boidae--Juvenile literature.   [1. Boa constrictor.
2. Snakes.]
I. Title.
QL666.O63M38   1996
597.96--dc20   95-45347
                                CIP
                                AC

It is a beautiful, sunny day in the Amazon rain forest of Brazil. The jungle is alive with sounds—birds singing, monkeys calling, insects buzzing. You see a bunch of green bananas hanging from a tree branch. Several birds are hopping around in the tree. The birds are looking for bugs to eat. Suddenly one of the birds squawks! It looks as if it is tangled up in a vine.

You look more closely. That bunch of green bananas was really an *emerald tree boa*. The snake had been waiting patiently on the branch. When one of the birds got too close, the tree boa grabbed it for its supper!

Emerald tree boas look like green bananas hanging on a branch.

WHERE DO BOAS LIVE?

The boa family has many members. Most boas live in the **New World**. The New World is made up of North America and South America. Thirty different kinds, or **species**, of boas live in the New World. Smaller boas, called *sand boas*, live in Europe and North Africa. Several other kinds of boas live on islands in the South Pacific and on the island of Madagascar. Boas can be found in tropical rain forests, swamps, along rivers, in the mountains, and even in dry, sandy areas.

Anacondas live along rivers, streams, and lakes in South America.

A boa's body is covered with thousands of scales. Most of the scales are small. On its belly, the boa has larger scales, called **scutes**. Boas have a skeleton made up of a skull, a long backbone and hundreds of ribs. Boas also have a heart, stomach, and two lungs.

A boa's body is covered with scales.

HOW BIG DO BOAS GROW?

Boas are some of the largest snakes in the world. The *common boa constrictor* can grow to be eighteen feet long. The *river anaconda*, a South American boa, can reach a length of thirty feet.

Boas are some of the largest snakes in the world.

Anacondas are the heaviest snakes in the world. An adult anaconda weighs at least 200 pounds. The biggest anaconda ever weighed was almost 600 pounds!

Some snakes lay eggs, just as birds do. Boas, however, give birth to squirming, wiggling little baby snakes. The young snakes grow inside the mother. Each baby snake lives in its own soft, clear egg. The babies get food from the egg yolk, just as a baby chicken does. When they are ready, the eggs "hatch" inside the mother's body. By the time they are born, the baby snakes are ready to eat and live on their own.

A boa constrictor can give birth to between thirty and fifty babies all at the same time. A large anaconda can have almost seventy babies at one time!

Like *garter snakes*, baby boas are ready to live on their own at birth.

WHAT DO BOAS EAT?

Boas eat many different kinds of animals. The animals they eat are called their **prey**. Large boas eat everything from small rodents and lizards to bigger birds and even alligators. Sometimes, anacondas eat pigs, dogs, or sheep!

Tree-climbing, or **arboreal**, boas eat lizards, birds, squirrels, and monkeys. Some arboreal boas have a very special diet. The *Cuban boa* and the *rainbow boa* love to eat bats!

The arms and legs of an animal fold down flat as the snake swallows .

Boas don't go out hunting for their prey. Instead, they wait for their prey to come to them. Large boa constrictors wait beside waterholes or paths. Anacondas lie in the shallow waters of lakes, streams, or rivers. Arboreal boas look like branches as they wait patiently among the leaves in a tree.

Boa constrictors wait by paths and waterholes for animals.

To "hear," boas put their heads flat against the ground or on a branch. They don't have any ears on the outside of their heads. Instead, they use their jawbones to feel movement, or **vibrations**, as their prey comes close. These jawbones carry the vibrations to an ear inside the snake's head. In this way, the boa "hears" its prey coming.

A boa listens by putting its head flat against a branch.

When the animal is close enough, the boa suddenly comes to life. The snake lunges forward and grabs the animal with its mouth. Boas have six rows of very sharp teeth. These teeth are curved backwards in the snake's mouth. The teeth help to grab the animal and hold on to it.

Boas have teeth that curve backwards, just like these python teeth

Next, the boa quickly wraps its body around the animal. Boas kill their prey by squeezing, or **constricting** it. That is why some boas are called boa constrictors. Every time the animal breathes out, the boa squeezes a little more. Soon the animal can't breathe at all.

After the animal stops breathing, the boa releases its deadly grip. Boas eat their food whole. The boa opens its mouth wide and slowly swallows its prey headfirst.

Boas squeeze their prey until the animal can't breathe anymore.

A boa can swallow an animal that is much bigger than its own head! How does it open its mouth wide enough to do this? The boa can make its upper and lower jaws come completely apart. It can also split its chin right down the middle. After the snake is done swallowing, its mouth returns to normal size.

Boas can separate their jaws to swallow large animals.

Snakes are an important part of the natural world. They eat lots of animals, such as mice and rats, that can become real pests! Many of the world's snake species are in danger of dying out, or becoming **extinct**. People can help the giant snakes survive by not buying anything made from snakeskin, and by supporting efforts to preserve the places where the snakes live.

Snakes are an important part of the natural world.

GLOSSARY

arboreal (ar-BOR-ee-ull)
Living in trees. Arboreal boas are boas that live in trees.

constrict (kon-STRICKT)
Squeeze tightly. Boas kill an animal by squeezing, or constricting, it so tightly that it cannot breathe.

extinct (ex-TINCKT)
No longer living. An animal that has died out—like the dinosaurs.

New World (NU wurld)
North and South America, including the United States. The Old World includes Africa, Asia, and Europe.

prey (PRAY)
An animal that is eaten by another animal. Boas eat many different kinds of prey.

scutes (scootz)
Large scales on the belly of a boa. The boa has scutes on its belly.

species (SPEE-sheez)
A separate kind of an animal. There are many different kinds, or species, of boas.

vibrations (vy-BRAY-shuns)
Feelings of movement. A boa rests its jawbone on the ground or on a branch to feel the movements of nearby animals.

INDEX